The Big Book of Giant Animals

Introduction

Animals always attract attention, sometimes because they have bright colors, sometimes for their strange or threatening appearance, or even because they do curious things. But the most surprising are the enormous ones. We all know that a long time ago, Earth was inhabited by gigantic animals like the dinosaurs that today, have disappeared. But other giants roam around us. Who are they? They live in forests, meadows, swamps and mountains all over the world; they are much larger than humans, and some are even larger than trees, boats, and houses.

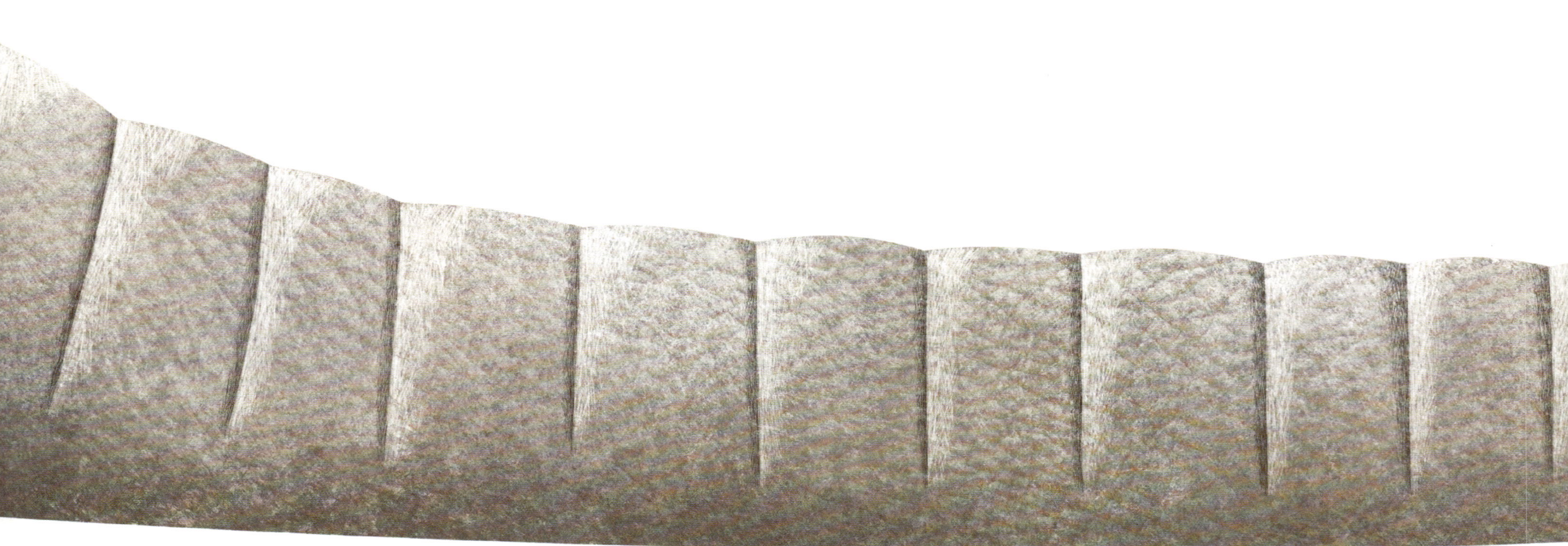

The larger an animal is, the more it needs to eat, so the places that are home to the giants of the Earth must be able to guarantee them large quantities of food: the savannas and prairies, for example, have such an abundance of grass that they are able to provide enough daily meals for many huge herbivores, like the elephant and the bison.

The sea is also a suitable place for hosting enormous creatures such as whales, not only because of the abundance of food, but also because the water supports the weight of their bodies, making them, despite their size, agile and almost graceful.

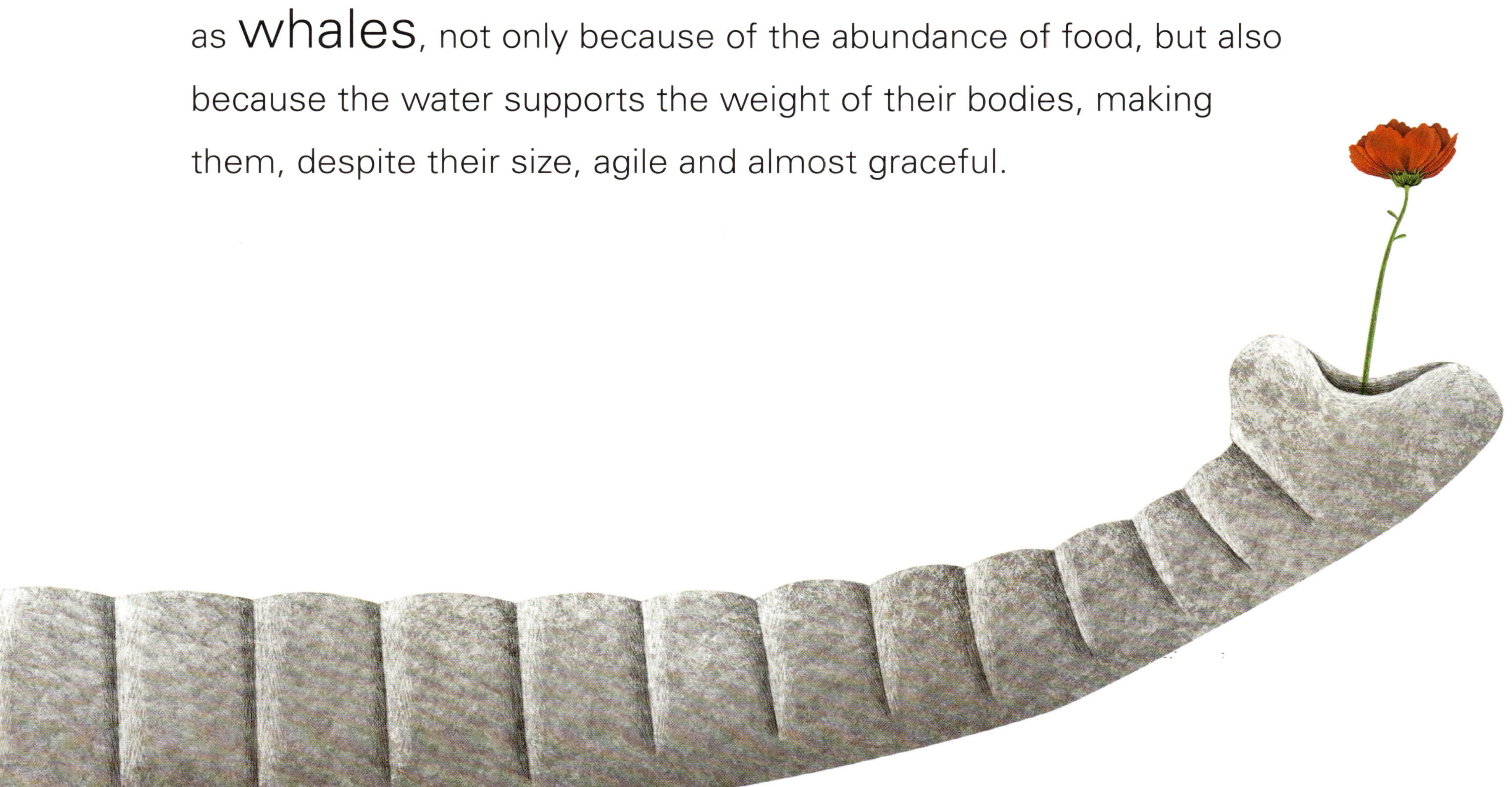

The **world's largest animal**, the blue whale, lives in the depths of the seas and the oceans but must surface regularly to breathe. Whales, in fact, **are not fish!** They breathe just like humans, **thanks to their lungs**, even though they are not able to hold their breath for very long: about a half an hour. The blue whale does not have teeth, but rather has **baleen plates** (which can be up to 11.5 feet (3.5 m) long!), which it uses as a comb to filter food out of the water. Blue whales make long migratory journeys, traveling from the cold waters of the North and South Poles to the warmer ones close the Equator, where they give birth to their offspring.

At 108 feet (33 m) long, it is the largest animal in the world!

Even its tongue is record-breaking at 20 feet (6 m) long!

Blue Whale

The African Elephant is more than 10 feet (3 m) tall.
African Elephant

The African elephant is not only the **largest** land animal, but **weighing 11 tons (10 t), it is definitely also the heaviest one!** It lives in Africa, both in the forests and in the arid savanna, where the climate is scorching. To lower their body temperature, elephants have developed an ingenious trick: flapping their **big ears!** It has a **long trunk** and two precious ivory teeth called **tusks**. Elephants live in small groups made up of females and baby elephants, guided by an elderly matriarch, while males prefer to live alone.

Elephant seals are large seals that live in the icy regions around the South Pole. Males are easily recognizable because they are 5 times larger than females and have a strange inflatable nose similar to a small trunk. They spend most of their life in the open sea, but come to the beach to reproduce. During this season, there are fierce fights between seals using their chests to conquer territory and the attention of females. Baby seals are covered with thick fur destined to disappear early in their lives as it is not well-suited for swimming.

The largest of the seals, the elephant seal is 16 feet (5 m) long.

Elephant Seal

Ostrich

An ostrich egg weighs 3 pounds (1.5 kg): this is also a record!

The ostrich is the **largest bird in the world**. Its body, except for its legs and neck, is covered in large, very soft feathers, but which are **not suitable for flying**. Not being able to use its wings to escape predators has made the ostrich a **very fast runner** It lives in Africa in habitats with little water, such as savannas, where it collects the **seeds, leaves and fruit** that are its favorite food. The male helps its partner incubate the eggs, laid inside a large **nest dug into the ground**, and, when they hatch, it will be the male that looks after and protects the chicks.

The giraffe inhabits the arid savannas of Africa. Of the animals that live on Earth today, it is surely **the tallest** because of its long legs and incredible neck that, strangely, is made up of only **7 bones**, just like ours! Its tongue is also very long to allow it to pick its favorite food: the **leaves of thorny acacias**. The giraffe moves with a strange, swaying movement that is very fast: its thin legs allow it to make **17 foot (5 m) long strides**.

Giraffe

Anaconda

The green anaconda lives in the wetlands of South America's tropical forests, like the Amazon rainforest, and **loves to swim** in fresh water, from which it attacks careless animals that approach the water to have a drink. **It is not a poisonous snake** and therefore kills its prey by suffocating

it with its muscular body before swallowing them whole, thanks to a flexible mouth that **can open to an exaggerated size**: snakes do not have teeth for chewing. The digestion of an **entire body** obviously takes a long time: **several weeks or even a few months!**

The saltwater crocodile has 64-68 teeth and is the largest reptile in the world.

Thanks to its **20 foot (6 m) length**, it is considered the largest reptile in our world. It lives in the swamps and rivers of North Australia and Southeast Asia. It is a **fierce predator** which generally hunts by ambush: it **lies motionless in the water** or near the shore, patiently waiting for an unknowing animal to approach and then it grabs it with its powerful jaws filled with **sharp teeth**, dragging it into the water, where it can enjoy its meal with complete calm. Saltwater crocodiles are **expert swimmers** and can move around in the open sea, even at long distances from the coast.

Saltwater Crocodile

As it is a shark and not a whale, it is considered the **largest fish in the world**. It is an innocuous giant that lives in warm seas all over Earth where the microscopic marine animals and tiny algae that it eats can be found in abundance. It swims just beneath the surface of the water, sucking large amounts of water into its wide, gaping mouth, where **310 rows of tiny teeth** that are not actually used for eating can be found. The whale shark is a **very slow swimmer** and it lets itself be approached without fear.

The whale shark is the largest fish in the world,
it is over 40 feet (23 m) long and its mouth is 5 feet (1.5 m) wide.

Whale Shark

The largest invertebrate in the world, it is 50 feet (15 m) long.

Colossal Squid

The colossal squid wins the record as the largest living invertebrate in the world. The female is larger than the male. It lives in the gloomy abysmal waters of the seas that flow around Antarctica and, in order to move and hunt in the dark, it is capable of producing light. In spite of its size, it has many predators, including the sperm whale: it is not uncommon to find pieces of this squid in the stomach of this whale. Like all squid, it has a beak that it uses to chop up its prey, usually other squid or small fish. Even today, the colossal squid is not well-known to scientists.

Polar bears are the largest carnivorous animals in the world.

Polar Bear

An animal from cold areas, the polar bear is considered the **largest carnivore on land**. It lives in Earth's icy Northern regions, moving across the frozen sea and following the migration patterns of the **seal**, its favorite prey.

Polar bears do not fear the cold because they are protected by **thick white fur** and a thick layer of **skin fat**. Babies are born during the dark, cold polar winter in a pit dug by the mother into the snow. They are completely helpless and need to be taken care of for a long time before they can leave the lair.

Hippopotamus

The hippopotamus is a large African herbivore that lives **in rivers and lakes**. It passes its days lazily, completely immersed in the water, with only its **eyes** and **ears**, found on the top of its head, sticking out. At night, it ventures onto land looking for grass that it eats in large quantities. Don't be misled by its seemingly good-nature: hippopotamuses are **very aggressive and dangerous**. Their large mouth contains two big canines similar to tusks, which they put on display as a sign of dominance. Each female gives birth to only one baby that is born underwater.

The white rhinoceros can run at speeds of up to 31 miles per hour (50 km/h).
White Rhinoceros

One of the giants of the African savannas, it is easily recognizable by the presence of **two large horns on its snout** that, unlike the real horns of buffaloes or goats, are made of the same material as fingernails and hair. Rhinoceroses eat grass that they collect using their muscular square lip, and then break up into little pieces with their molars, the only teeth they have. Rhinoceroses are not sharp-sighted, but they **have exceptional hearing and sense of smell**. The female gives birth to one baby at a time, which remains with the mother until it is three years old.

Moose

It is the largest member of the deer family and is recognizable, aside from its size, for its large muzzle and horns, more properly called antlers, **resembling large blades** and that only the males have. Moose inhabit the wooded areas rich in rivers, lakes and swamps of North America and Northern Europe. They love to be immersed in water, even completely, and **are skilled swimmers**. Once a year, males lose their antlers and then re-grow them in a short time slightly larger than the ones lost. Like deer, moose also **fight one another** to conquer territory and win the attention of females.

The wingspan of the Andean condor measures 10 feet (3 m).
Andean Condor

It is one of the largest birds in the world capable of flying. The Andean condor lives in the mountains, but also along the coasts of South America, where strong currents rising upwards help sustain its weight while in flight. As a member of the vulture family, it is a scavenger and helps to clean up the environment: it actually eats dead animals, which it easily picks clean with its robust beak. Its head and neck are completely featherless so that it does not get dirty while eating. Males have a fleshy crest.

It is the largest monkey in the world and lives in central Africa, both in the forests of the plains and in those found in the mountains. It is a very intelligent animal. Families are made up of females with small children and a single adult male that leads and protects them, defending them from leopards, men and other gorillas, even at the cost of its own life. On a normal day, gorillas move around the forest, rest and eat. Their favorite foods are leaves, soft shoots, twigs, roots, fruit and even insects.

The world's largest monkey weighs about 400 pounds (180kg).
Gorilla

Ocean sunfish are the largest and heaviest fish in the world with a bone skeleton. It is an awkward swimmer because of the shape of its body that is flattened sideways and rounded, reminiscent of the sun, and from which it gets its name. Ocean sunfish live in the open sea in the temperate and tropical waters of oceans all over the world and is a predator to jellyfish, which it eats in great quantities. Its mouth is very small and never completely closes; its teeth are fused together to form a kind of beak.

The ocean sunfish has skin that is 6 inches (15 cm) thick and a body that is 10 feet (3 m) long.
Ocean Sunfish

The bison is the largest mammal in North America.

The bison is the largest mammal in North America and lives on large prairies where it can find plenty of grass to eat. Its body is covered in **long, thick brown fur,** which insulates it and protects it both from heat in the summer and snow and frost in the winter. Although it has a large, massive body, the bison is quite **fast and very agile** and is able to make high jumps or change direction quickly while running. Bisons are not sharp-sighted, but they hear noises easily and have a good sense of smell.

American
Bison

This huge sea turtle is very special because it has a shell (called carapace) not made of bone, but rather of skin as hard as leather with multiple rows of ridges crossing it. It swims in seas all over the world, making long trips and diving up to 3000 feet (1000 m) deep to chase jellyfish that it eats in large quantities. Like all sea turtles, the female leatherback sea turtle builds a nest on a sandy beach so as not to ruin its delicate carapace shell on the rocks.

It is the largest invertebrate in the world and reaches up to 4.9 feet (1.5 m) in length.

Leatherback Sea Turtle

Francesca Cosanti attended the Multimedia Illustration and Animation Course at Istituto Europeo di Design in Rome, an illustration course at Officina b5 - Accademy of Illustration in Rome and various intensive illustration courses with famous international illustrators. She has been working as an illustrator for publishers, advertising firms, associations, companies and agencies since 2005. She also teaches in various schools as an expert in illustration, drawing techniques, graphic design and multimedia software. In the past years, she has illustrated several books for White Star Kids, with great enthusiasm and creativity.

WSKids
WHITE STAR KIDS

White Star Kids® is a registered trademark property of White Star s.r.l.

Piazzale Luigi Cadorna, 6 - 20123 Milan, Italy
www.whitestar.it

Translation: TxTradurre

ISBN 978-88-544-1273-6
2 3 4 5 6 22 21 20 19 18

Printed in China